# 4 MARRIAGES BEFORE 40

## Mistakes, Hurt, Love, and Discovery

### *A Memoir*

## BY: TAKENYA MIMS

Misty,

I appreciate your support! I pray my story inspires you in some way. Happy Reading!

Copyright © 2020 by Takenya Mims

Published by Takenya Mims in Partnership with
The Literary Revolutionary

The Literary Revolutionary & Co

www.theliteraryrevolutionary.com

Editing By: Anjé McLish
Cover Design By: Opeyemi Ikuborije

**Manufactured in the United States of America**

ISBN #: 978-1-950279-31-9

# 4 MARRIAGES BEFORE 40

## Mistakes, Hurt, Love, and Discovery

### *A Memoir*

## BY: TAKENYA MIMS

# DEDICATION

This book is for those who are tired of the same Cycle

For those who have ever felt Uncertain

For those who need to find their source of Powerlessness

For those who believe that everything happens for a Reason

For those who internally hold on to Pain

For those who refuse to Give up

For those who believe in the power of Redemption

For those who believe in God

To Hazen, my heart, my love, my wake-up call for living:
Auntie loves you with all her might! I will forever be
grateful to God for blessing my life with you!

To my best friends/sisters who pushed me, loved me,
offered listening ears, offered strong shoulders, valued our
bond, told me when I was wrong, and consistently
encouraged and motivated me — Sydrea, LaQuesha,
Bridgette, & Tracy! I love you ladies to the moon!

"For everything there is a season, and a time for every purpose under heaven:  a time to be born, and a time to die; a time to plant, and a time to pluck up that which is planted;  a time to kill, and a time to heal; a time to break down, and a time to build up;  a time to weep, and a time to laugh; a time to mourn, and a time to dance;  a time to cast away stones, and a time to gather stones together;  a time to embrace, and a time to refrain from embracing;  a time to seek, and a time to lose; a time to keep, and a time to cast away;  a time to rend, and a time to sew; a time to keep silence, and a time to speak;  a time to love, and a time to hate; a time for war, and a time for peace."

**Ecclesiastes 3:1-8 (ASV)**

# CONTENTS

# FOREWORD

Tears rolled down her face as she was surrounded by some of the greatest young preachers in Memphis. They were there to support her. They were there to show her love after her husband and their preacher friend was laid to rest. She sat at the head table, a place often reserved for ministers and ministers' wives during celebrations in the huge reception room at St. Mark church. However, this time, there was no true celebration—we were at the repast following the funeral of her late, 25-year-old husband, Stewart. We were all young and innocent until that moment. Life changed and tragedy was introduced on a scale we never could have imagined or processed.

The tears that marked her red-rimmed eyes probably never really ceased falling. I wanted to hug her without letting go. Yet, she was still scarred and bruised herself, not only emotionally but physically. I never knew how strong she was and how fragile, too, until that moment. She was my sister, but I could no longer truly feel her pain. We had shared laughs for years and songs of joy, but I could no longer resonate with her distress. Her suffering was out of my reach. I could see her hurting and could do nothing to stop it.

I knew that soon the crowds would slowly start their reverse tide. She would get fewer calls consoling her and fewer stops by the house just to visit or bring her thoughtful gifts. Fewer people to offer condolences in her new role as a widow. I knew that she would soon have to forge her own way: a new way, a new life. She would have to figure out who she was. No longer a preacher's wife, or a pastor's wife, or simply a wife. She was just her.

She was never one to wear makeup or any sort of cover at all, but it was as if she presented herself even more firmly now. She bore herself—scars and all. Every cut and bruise that marked her skin after the fatal accident, she bore with courage. They were symbols of what she had been through. She didn't hide from her new reality. She forged her way through. Her wounds were a testimony of what she had lost. But what did she have to gain?

Months went by and years steamrolled past. She smiled again. She laughed. She made new friends. She returned to school. She learned new recipes. She signed new leases. She traveled. She experimented with her looks. She re-entered the game of love. She sought her purpose. And here we are, a whole book later, and you can see that she is still standing. Or should I say, you will see. She is still pursuing. She is still embracing. She is still Takenya. Life gave her more roadblocks than many, and yet, she still managed to maneuver each one.

Takenya will take you on a journey in this book. A journey through her life. And if you truly knew how private she is, you would be remiss to not sit back and enjoy the ride! She shares not only who she is, but how she got here. How she went from wife to wife to widow to more than she ever knew. She is my sister and, even though I lived and watched the journey with her, she made me realize through this book that not only does she have more in her than I ever knew but she is probably the most deserving of love; true love. That once-in-a-lifetime love that you can miss in 4 marriages but find in yourself along the way.

She taught me that it's not the person you're with, but the person you are.


- Tracy Walker, *Baby Sister and Admirer*

# INTRO

## MY SENSE OF EMOTION

I was born the first of three. If I must say so myself, I was a cutie pie. I did, however, start wearing glasses in fourth grade. Standing close to the TV for so long had finally taken an effect. I hated wearing glasses, and I will never forget my first pair. They were like a clear pink tint and the frames were shaped as octagons. Sheesh! My favorite shoes were my pink and white LA Gear high-tops. What a sight! My parents used to have us in reading programs growing up, so I developed a love for books, and it is still one of my favorite hobbies. With that came my love for writing. I used to find notebooks and just freely write, mainly when I locked myself in my room, which was a lot. At the age of 11 or 12, I received a diary as a gift and that prompted me to express my feelings with words even more. My pen and paper were my best friend.

I was very quiet in school. For the most part, I was kind of shy. I didn't fully open up to people outside of family until about sixth grade. Once I got into seventh grade, I was boy crazy. I lived for their attention, mainly because I didn't feel wanted at home. Home life was picture perfect, but honestly I didn't like it. We were at church so much that I began to dread it. Throughout my life it became such a routine that I used to vow that when I got grown, I wasn't going anymore. We went to Sunday School, morning worship, Baptist Training Union (BTU), and Sunday night service. If we had a 3:00 program we went to those as well. We went to every revival, vacation bible school (VBS), youth congress meeting, etc. Even thinking about these things in hindsight, they would have been okay had there been a family and church-life balance, but there wasn't. Church was the priority in the house; we had so many rules and I was always in trouble for something. We had Bible study every day and night at home. We couldn't watch anything that wasn't Black or Disney. I rebelled against so many things and began to seclude myself whenever we were at home. I always felt as if church was more important to my parents than us growing a personal bond, learning about them and their upbringings, feeling free to address my emotions and thoughts, and even talking about sex. I didn't really know who they were besides the obvious, simply my parents.

I had my few church friends that I grew up with who were my only friends until sixth grade. I began to spend time with one girl, but never let many into my personal space. It was something about girls that I didn't really like. Maybe they talked too much or were just annoying. But once I hit seventh grade, all I wanted to hang around were boys. I even began to dress like them by wearing baggy clothes. I used to sneak and wear my dad's clothes to school and change before he would get home. Everyone that got to know me personally liked me. I was easy to talk to once I accepted you into my world. I cared for those around me, sometimes too hard or too soon. A lot of times, that came back to bite me in the ass.

♥

I would like to think my sense of emotion began to shift for good once I became a senior in high school. This particular night I was sneaking out of the house to meet with someone I trusted for a physical escapade. We went to school together and I had known him since Jr. high. From 7$^{th}$ to12$^{th}$ grade, we developed a physical bond like no other. He was my way of feeling good and feeling wanted when I needed attention. He made me feel so special, like I was the only one he craved. He was possessive and I liked it. Having sex had unknowingly become my source of self-confidence. At that time, it never dawned on me that boys were severely selfish and only looked out for themselves. I thought I was wanted and desired, but boy was I wrong!

This particular night, he picked me up and we went to another classmate's house. I was unaware that this was where we were going, but I rolled with it. We walked into the house and there were more classmates of ours, each one I knew by name. I spoke and followed him to the back of the house. We went into a room and began to do what I got out of the house for. Afterward, he walked out, and I got up to get re-dressed. My clothes were gone. He took them. Now I was beginning to panic, so I paced, looking again to make sure I didn't overlook them. Nothing was there. I slightly opened the door, called his name, and closed it shut. Seconds later, the door opened, but it was not him. I asked my classmate, "What are you doing here?" While walking towards me, he leaned forward and said, "He'll be back, what's up with you?" I said nothing because I was trying to cover up and keep calm, but within the blink of an eye my legs were open, and I was on my back. I was laying in tears and after he finished, he walked out while zipping his pants back up. I found my voice and yelled, "Tell him to come here!" Before the door closed back, in walked another classmate. At this point, I felt myself getting emotional, like I wanted to die. He tried the same approach as the previous person but thankfully, he stopped mid-sentence, looked at me, and walked back out the door. He returned with my clothes in his hands.

I hurriedly got dressed and walked out of the room pissed, ashamed, betrayed, and hurt. How could someone I trusted for so many years treat me as if he just met me? We'd been messing around for about five years at that point. Did he ever care about me? It was obvious that I valued him way more than he valued me. He didn't give two shits about me or my feelings!

I was prepared to walk home and stormed past everyone, then a guy who was not involved met me outside and took me home. I secretly vowed to never speak to any of them again. I had never felt such a mixture of emotions like that in my life, but I had to shake it off because we had school the next day. That night, my mental state began shifting to becoming emotionless and nonchalant. I no longer cared what men thought or what they wanted. I would use them like they did me, with only my pleasure in mind.

# NICK

I met Nick after moving back home from Chicago in 2000. I was leaving Best Buy one day and he was going in with his friend. He was so handsome: brown-skinned, dressed nice, pretty brown eyes, and tall (well, taller than me). We were both looking at each other, so we exchanged numbers and started spending time together. He showed me so much attention, by us talking on a very consistent basis and spending quality time by going on dates and even visiting each other's church. He was and is still a preacher, so we had many enlightening conversations. Conversations of what it felt like to be a preacher at such a young age, how my dad was a preacher, and if he felt pressured to follow his dad's footsteps. He was a preacher's kid and so was I. Preacher's kids united!

We both loved God and spent a lot of time in church. We talked about the many services we used to attend, funny choir moments, etc. In addition to having so many church aspects in common, we also had sex in common. Boy, did we have sex in common. We went at it so much, I thought I was addicted. He made me feel wanted and that he had to have me. I didn't mind obliging because I, in return, needed him and he always made me feel desired.

We used to listen to Fred Hammond so much that I learned many of his songs within weeks. My parents adored Nick, and I loved his parents. I still remember that his dad used to call me Takenja, despite many corrections. So many memories.

After four months of constantly spending time and dating, we were married; I was 19 years old. Of course, I wasn't ready to get married, but I was ready to get away from my dad and his ridiculous rules. I hated being at home; I had crazy curfews and was told 'no' to so many things. Now, it could have been because I had just gotten back from running away from home and moving to Chicago with my boyfriend at the time. See, I had left right after high school graduation in '99. He was an older guy and very sweet. We worked together at Seessel's, an old grocery store in Memphis. I used to sneak out of the house all the time to be with him. One early morning, I came back home and the door was locked. I knew that my parents had seen I wasn't at home, so I just turned back around, got in the car with him, and left. Not too long after, he said he was moving back home and asked if I wanted to come. I said yes. I went home and packed two garbage bags full of clothes and left town. It was such an adventure.

I loved the weather and being with my boyfriend was super exciting. I felt like a grown lady, even though I was only 18 when we left town. We enjoyed a lot of the same things and he made me feel safe. I didn't have any worries whenever he was around. I was comfortable in knowing that he would take care of me. A month or so after being in Chicago, his family was having a cookout, so we were all outside. We were having a good time when all of a sudden, a sheriff's department car pulled up. There was another car behind it as well. The door opened and there stood my dad. I thought," How in the world did he find me?" I immediately got scared and froze in my seat. My dad walked up and greeted my boyfriend's parents and then spoke to me. He stated that he wanted me to come home and, for a split second, I thought I had to until his mom spoke and said, "You don't have to leave if you don't want to. You are of age to decide." After hearing this, I found my voice and told him I was staying.

After living with his parents for a few months, we got our own place, and I even started working for a while at Target. Over time, my feelings began to change, and I began to miss what was so familiar, no matter how much I disliked the surroundings. I wanted to go back home, so we talked about it and he drove me back to Memphis. He stayed in town and we got another place together, but it didn't last long. I eventually moved back in with my parents. Despite the turmoil I may have caused, they welcomed me back with open and loving arms. A few months later I met Nick.

Nick spoiled me despite myself. Nick and I explored a lot with each other, and it was fun to do. I used to dream of being a housewife, and with Nick I could be one. I kept the house clean and cooked while he worked to provide for the both of us. We didn't have any kids, so I used to spoil animals: hamsters and guinea pigs. We had a great time together when we dated and even during our marriage, when I wasn't being difficult. We created such a bond of friendship that we enjoyed simple things with each other. We were both homebodies, so a lot of our days were spent chilling at home or seeing family members. We physically separated a lot during the marriage; I would leave and move back home for a few months then come back to him. Every time I left, it was mainly because I would feel trapped and wanted to step out and cheat. I was battling with myself to be faithful and I would lose that battle very often. It was a repeated cycle for so long. At one point, he even roomed with my uncle while we were apart. After reconciling during one period, I moved in with them. It was such a funhouse.

Nick loved me and he showed me by how he took care of me. I loved him in return, but I was nowhere near ready to be in any type of committed relationship. I played around and had no sense of remorse. That selfish mindset was rearing its ugly head again. I did what I wanted. I wanted my cake and I had to eat it too.

Life was great with Nick; I never had a reason to question his love or faithfulness. However, my rebellious side was lying in wait and it was beginning to itch. I started talking to other men and cheating left and right for no reason other than my own pleasure. It wasn't a mind-blowing pleasure that I was seeking. At that age, I had no idea of anything past simple sex. I'd never heard of an orgasm at this point. The pleasure I sought or missed was simply having choices. Being committed was such a struggle for me and instead of turning down men's advances, I challenged them. Reflecting on those times showed me that I was an immature ass. I didn't care about anyone's feelings but my own. We separated off and on for the next three years, and I finally called it quits in 2004. During those years we fought and argued constantly. I was back and forth from living with him and living with my parents. I could not whole-heartedly reciprocate love or be faithful.

Nick fought for us; he didn't want us to end, but I couldn't continue to string him along. If I wanted out, I had to do it myself because he refused to give up. It takes two people in a relationship to make it work, and I was emotionally detached and had no fight to give. I wasn't feeling the commitment anymore, mainly because initially I wasn't really ready to be in something as serious as marriage. After all, I was super young and not completely knowledgeable about the role of being a wife and everything that it entailed. Being faithful, being presently available, being open to discussing problems successfully. I was talking to other men, so my focus was not solely on Nick. I didn't know how to work through conflict in a loving manner. All of this had eventually become mentally draining. I couldn't continue down this path of self-destructing and firsthand continuing to destroy his trust and our foundation of friendship. I didn't see the point of holding on anymore; I just couldn't get myself on the right path emotionally. So, being tired of going back and forth, I decided to file for divorce.

I celebrated with a threesome as soon as I left court for the final hearing, go figure!

In contrast to how our marriage ended, we remained in contact and cordial with one another. He was my confidant and best friend. We actually still saw each other afterward from time to time. I had always known that he truly cared for my well-being and that was amazing because I knew that I had hurt him repeatedly over the years. He showed me what it felt like to be loved unconditionally and what it meant to truly forgive someone. I always admired his heart and love for people, whether in close proximity or someone he randomly met. Despite everything I selfishly did to him and our marriage, he still cared. His compassion and love for me was one that I will always remember and appreciate.

♥

A few months after the divorce, I moved out of my parent's house and got my first apartment with my cousin. Talk about freedom. I was uber excited! A few months after moving away from home, we got the unexpected news that my grandmother passed away. My soul shook that day. I will never forget my mom telling me and my sister and all I could do was slide to the floor, scream and cry.

Grandma Peaches had always been my rock. I talked to her several times before I talked to my parents (if I even talked to them at all). She loved God and that was vividly clear in her walk and her talk. She gave me such good advice about marriage and knew about my love for Nick. She asked me hard questions all the time and made sure I knew that she loved me.

She always had encouraging words to give; she never made me feel like I disappointed her. She always expressed genuine love. You could tell she loved God with all her might. Losing Grandma Peaches made me feel like I had lost my best friend. She always showed me love, talked to me, could see when something was wrong with me, cooked my favorite dishes, and held me when I cried. I never felt like the "black sheep" around her. I always felt included and like my feelings mattered.

I learned to cook a few of her dishes before she passed and for that I am grateful. I don't know anyone that can make cornbread, fish, jelly cake, pound cake, greens, or smothered potatoes like she did. Her funeral was in Greenville, Mississippi, which is where she resided. There were so many people there. Even our church in Memphis - St. Mark took a bus to MS to show support and love for her life and for us. Unforgettable.

Her name was my first and most cherished tattoo. I still think of her!

# STEWART

I don't know if it is just my upbringing or just being in the family that I'm in, but I've always had some sort of connection to preachers. Nick was a preacher, so when we got married, I became my mother and grandmother; a preacher's wife. I didn't know or grasp the full concept of the role personally, but I had two close role models.

The summer of 2004, my sister invited me to go hear her boyfriend preach one night, and I saw "him". I asked her who he was, and she told me his name was Stewart, which I later found out was his last name. I was physically smitten by him, and guess what? He was a preacher. We didn't verbally talk that night but about a month later, there he was at my church. We used to have gospel explosions during youth month in September, where different groups and choirs came to sing or perform. He was there to sing with this young preacher's group he was a member of called Men of Distinction. After service that night, he walked up to me and we started talking. I was older than him by three years, so I wasn't really taking a lot of what he said seriously. He would talk about him being a preacher, the things he had, what he wanted to learn about me, how he found me attractive, and other things that made me feel like it was just a lot of hot air to a certain extent. A group of us went to Applebee's for a late dinner and I invited him to my place afterward. That Sunday was the beginning of a lifetime—or so I thought.

We became inseparable. We spent so much time together, you couldn't see him without me and vice versa. I used to go with him and support him like a good girlfriend whenever he had to preach. He had such a wonderful delivery with preaching and boy, could he sing. He was a quartet singer down to his soul and never preached a sermon without singing a song before or after.

Needless to say, we saw each other so much that he ended up moving in with me. Sounds crazy, but we were attached. I didn't expect to, but I fell in love with him. We were such kindred spirits when it came to church and music. We enjoyed every moment we were able to spend together. He was very aggressive and possessive, which was such a turn on to me. Every time he had to preach he would ask me to come. Sometimes he wouldn't even ask; he would just tell me. I felt like he wanted and needed my support, and I was very willing to give it to him. As time passed, we had several rough patches, and I noticed that he had a bad temper. We were never physical with each other, so I didn't let it bother me.

In 2005, he proposed but I told him he had to wait. I didn't want to make the same mistake twice in marrying too fast, so we made the choice to do it in May of 2006 when I would be 25. It was a very informal ceremony at my grandfather's church, but we promised each other to do it big at a later date.

One characteristic about Stewart was his old soul. Being raised by his grandparents, he was an old, traditional man at heart. He had a know-it-all attitude, and he felt like he always had to have the last word. He also wasn't very fond of new fashion or me having my own style of dress. He had the mindset of a woman having a certain place and not always having a say in decisions. He didn't like drastic things, which was crazy because when we met, I had at least two tattoos, cornrows in my head, and a tongue ring. I wasn't quiet-spoken, so when I had an opinion, you would know it. We

25

seemed so different on the outside, but we were severely attached to each other.

One distinct trait about him that caused many conflicts was his controlling nature. When we started dating, there were so many things he tried to change about me; my hair, the way I dressed, piercings, etc. The bad thing was I let him. Why did I do that? I questioned myself several times. I loved him with all of me, but did he genuinely love me? In my opinion, if someone is attempting to change things about you that make you who you are, then how are they truly accepting all of you? He used to tell me that since he was a preacher, I had to act and dress like I was with one. So, I humbly obliged. I didn't like that I had to change to be with someone and we argued about it but because of his stance and his place in my life, I made the changes he requested.

Gradually, I began to lose sight of myself for his sake. That was a sad space to be in, but I did it because of my love and commitment to him. I was committed to what we had and wanted to show that I believed in him and in us. I loved him hard, sometimes more than myself. Once we got married, he started controlling my relationships with my friends. He did not want me talking to them or socializing with them anymore. To this day, I still don't understand why. He made those demands with no explanation. After a while, if they were not immediate family, we only hung around his friends.

This was so heartbreaking to me because when we first dated, I was rooming with my cousin. Then, after she left, my best friend Sydrea moved in with me. During our lease together, Stewart slowly moved in with us in my room. She witnessed our early ups and downs, yet never judged the circumstance. For him to try and pull me away from those closest to me was absurd. I always cherished my friends and family. They were there before him, so why should I get rid of them? They were my support system, and it felt as if he didn't want me to have my own circle of support and love. I tried to understand it, but I never got a clear answer except control. I had a conversation with my friends and even though they hated what was happening, they respected my dilemma.

Even though my time was forcefully becoming shortened with my friends, the times we did have together were so important. During the early months of our marriage in 2006, there was an event that took place that changed my life. My best friend, Bridgette, asked me to do something that I never fathomed. It was a Sunday afternoon after church, and she invited me over for dinner. It was nothing unusual because we always ate together, especially on Sundays. Well, this day was special. She and her husband Dre invited me and his best friend over to eat. While eating Bridgette got serious and started talking about me and our friendship and how she felt about me. She then proceeded to ask if I would be Kennedy's god mom. Kennedy is her first daughter, her and Dre's first child together.

I was so blown away that I couldn't do anything but cry. I was so honored to be asked to fill these shoes; I have always loved kids and desired to have my own. This was a role that I felt I was made for. I accepted while still crying and since then, I have done nothing but love Kennedy with all my heart. We spent so much time together, Kennedy and me. She filled my heart with more love and patience. I will never forget that day and what it meant to me.

♥

Within the next year, Stewart was called to pastor, so that meant I would become a first lady. I was so not prepared for that title, but I knew it would eventually happen, so here we were. We endured so many things at that church; fake people, deacons taking over, people asking for money, lack of support, members being two-faced, you name it. They weren't really looking for a pastor to lead them; they were looking for someone young to draw a crowd, preach, and go home. There was no respect given, no matter how much he obliged, did what they asked, and made himself available to their every need. After having many arguments, discussions, and heartbreaking moments, Stewart resigned in 2008.

That was so hard for him to do because it was something he was so passionate about. He knew most of the people there personally, and how they treated him broke his heart. Shortly after, Stewart had the idea to start a church. Most of the members that joined the church under him followed us when we left. They were asking to go wherever he preached and still wanted to take care of him. I wasn't initially on board with it because we couldn't afford to do it, financially. I also didn't genuinely feel that he was called to do something as big as that. I shared my concerns, but he didn't really care to listen to them.

Without much of a choice, he reached out to everyone and we began to hold services in our home. We even began merging with another pastor and his church on Sundays where he used to alternate preaching services. Having worship service at home and combining with the other church went well for a while as far as keeping everyone together and having great services. Then, it slowly began to fade away. Members began to miss service until they would eventually not come anymore. Some sought more stability, and he was beginning to preach at other churches a lot.

Later that same year, we hit a rough patch within our marriage where I felt like I needed to leave. I was tired of not being heard, tired of following orders, tired of being dictated to, and tired of spending so much time with his friends while my personal friendships were quickly fading. He used to spend a lot of time with one preacher, hanging out, going to eat, even preached for him often. Eventually, he started making me tag along because his friend was married as well. We used to spend so much time with them that I began to despise even hearing their name. Every time we went over their house, it was like Stewart would forget we had a home, and we would always leave around midnight or later. He didn't care if I had to work nor did he respect my feelings about the situation. We did what he wanted, and I had to accept it. I gained so much weight during this period because all we would do was go to church, eat, stay up, and sleep.

One thing that irked my soul was how he used to compare our marriage to theirs. He would try to act like his friend and get mad and fuss at me because I didn't act like his wife. Well, his wife rarely spoke, and she did everything her husband asked her. She was a doormat to me, and it made me mad being around it. So, naturally I became offended when he would start comparing and tried to push our relationship in that same direction. After watching for so long, I noticed that he wanted to run everything, rarely listening to my suggestions. I had to be quiet and not question anything he did. He was doing what he saw his friend do and I was tired of having to explain that our marriage was not theirs. I made it clear that if he kept comparing and trying to mimic them, we weren't going to last.

Finally, I had reached my breaking point, so we separated, and I moved back home with my parents. During this time, I sought marital counseling because simply talking to him wasn't cutting it. He didn't listen to me or care about how I was feeling. The only other option in my eyes was to seek outside help. While I went seeking therapy for my marital issues, a deeper issue had surfaced. My issues with my parents, in particular my dad.

♥            .

This discovery threw me for a loop because, since the age of 12, I had suppressed anger, hurt, and disappointment. There were so many years of built-up tension that answering questions and having an honest discussion with a complete stranger made it vividly clear. I didn't realize that the resentment I was beginning to feel with Stewart was the same emotion I felt with my dad. He reminded me of my dad in the way of being controlled, not feeling emotionally free, and having so many rules to just be with him. At an early age, I pulled away from my parents because of never being able to do things right, not having constructive conversations with them, and not feeling as if I could trust them with my inner thoughts and struggles. Now, here I was feeling the same towards my husband.

Throughout our marriage, I discovered a lot of things about me as far as self-esteem, and how afraid I was to be honest about my feelings. Being truthful and vulnerable didn't seem like a smart thing to do. I never felt good enough and I was always nervous about being seen emotionally. Those feelings were rooted in my childhood, but at the time I had no idea where they stemmed from.

Stewart refused counseling, so I did it alone for a short period of time, then I stopped going altogether. During counseling, my father was brought in to confront the hurt I had in our relationship. Having my counselor in the room allowed me to feel safe enough to let my guard down and be honest. I eventually pulled away from counseling, but always knew that I could reach out to her at any moment. It felt good to let my dad in on some things, but it was sort of at surface level. The bigger issues were never discussed, like how I was affected by certain actions and how I suppressed a lot of my feelings instead of talking them out. There were still so many things left unsaid. My childhood issues were briefly addressed, but my marital issues were still at large.

May 25, 2008, while still separated, Stewart and I had an over 4-hour conversation discussing what our next step would be for our marriage. While discussing many issues, I confessed to an act of infidelity during our marriage while we were separated. Before I knew it, he was at my parent's front door. I was instantly afraid because I knew he was pissed off, but I was even more afraid of what would happen if I didn't go outside to the car like he kept demanding. So, I went outside. We sat in the car going back and forth with each other for a while, he snatched my phone away, then he pulled off. Half-dressed, because he made me get out of bed, and frightened, I asked where we were going but he never responded. He drove around the corner to an empty lot behind Home Depot, parked, and made me get out of the car. Shaking, I did what he asked. He demanded I get undressed and, once I did, he started slapping and punching me. I screamed and cried so loud, hoping someone would hear me while begging and pleading with him to stop, trying to convince him of how sorry I was.

Suddenly, he stopped hitting me, he made me put my clothes back on, and drove us away. I thought he was taking me back home, but he actually drove to our house in South Memphis. Once we got there, he started attacking and calling me out of my name again. I was in a headlock on the floor in our bedroom begging him to let me go, afraid for my life.

His brother was there. I had no idea until I looked up, pleading with my eyes and arms outstretched for help. He never moved.

Talking to Stewart did no good because if my response was not "Yes" or "I'm moving back home," something else happened to me. So eventually I just shut up. After I couldn't cry and fight anymore, he released me. I was forced to get into our bed, do my wifely duty, and go to sleep. The next day, I was given my phone back. I had to lie to my mom and tell her that I was okay. I called my sister to come pick me up. It hurt to lie because I really wanted to cry and express what really happened. But, in the back of my head, I felt as if the fingers would be pointed at me and I would be made to feel like I did it to myself. I also still wanted to protect him and not expose that side of him to her or my dad. My glasses were broken, my body was sore, and my heart was torn. Yet, I still felt like it was all my fault and that I deserved everything I got.

♥

He hounded me every day for weeks after that altercation until I agreed to speak with him. Over the course of 2 ½ months, we went back and forth with arguments, fighting, being frustrated with each other, and making up. He fought for us, getting my sister and our friend to persuade me to talk to him. But it showed me that he was not willing to just walk away. He loved me. He had forgiven my infidelity and I was willing to forgive him for his deeds and attempt to move forward. Him loving me despite my mistake showed me that he sincerely cared and that he acted out of hurt and anger. People don't always act or respond how we think they should when they've been wronged. To me, my infidelity was deep because he knew the person, so I accepted my part and forgave him for his.

By the end of June, we were back together. Everything was settled for the most part. But by February of 2009, we were back in the same space. I eventually left again in March and refused to go back until he sought counseling and learned to control his anger. By June I had made the decision to go back home to give us another try. Despite my bad choices and his temper, I missed him and deeply loved him. I needed him and I felt like he truly needed me. When we were apart, I felt like a huge chunk of my heart was missing. I missed his hugs and his singing around the house. I missed laying under him. I even missed proofreading his sermons and offering suggestions. I needed that love back, physically and emotionally. I needed to be close to him.

After I moved back home with him, I felt like I was with an entirely different man. Everything that pushed me out the door had changed. He was more attentive, understanding, he listened to me more, he asked instead of demanding things, and he was more active with showing love and affection. He didn't let outsiders like friends or family dictate our relationship; he stood up for me when it came to his family. They had issues with me that I never understood, and it was hard for him to see. After a while, he saw it for himself and did what he needed to do, which was stick by his wife. He made me feel necessary and whenever I was disrespected, he nipped it in the bud.

I had always loved him with all my heart but now, I was ecstatically in love. Everything was refreshing and new. We went on dates, we talked more, spent less time doing things just for him but participated in activities for both of us. It had finally clicked that it was about us and not them. I still felt as if he was my soulmate, and I was so glad that I decided to give us another try to get it right. I knew we had a lot of differences and several bad incidents, but I was so in love with him. To me, what was true love without going through some sort of pain? In our instance, I was the cause of a lot of pain and I, at those times, felt as if I deserved some of it. True love has never been easy; without a test, how do you know if you can trust it? I trusted what I felt and what he felt because we overcame and loved even harder after the battle!

# GRIEF

Time passed and everything within our marriage was on the upside. We were doing great, communicating, going out, and I had my personal relationships with my friends back. September 2, 2009 came around and my life took an unexpected halt. I was working at Rust College in Holly Springs, MS during that time, which was about 30-40 minutes from where we lived. It was a Tuesday morning because he had a minister's meeting to go to later that day. We had two cars at that time, and my car wouldn't crank. I was so mad and frustrated with that car because it had been causing problems for the past few months and we couldn't figure out what was going on with it. So, I had to wake him up and have him take me to work so he could keep the other car to get around throughout the day. He came out of the apartment with his PJs and house shoes on and jumped in the driver's seat.

We were on the road and driving down Lamar, and I pulled out my portable DVD player to watch the Golden Girls. I am a diehard fanatic! After watching an episode, we began to talk. I asked him to call my Uncle Robert and see if he could come look at the car while I was at work. He called and left a message on his machine for a callback. We then resumed talking and because I knew I had previously woke him up out of his sleep I asked, "Are you going to be okay going back home?" He replied, "Yeah, I'll be fine." Then everything went black.

When my eyes opened, I remembered everything being blurry, my glasses were gone. Why were we facing traffic? The car was facing oncoming traffic. I couldn't get my mind around what happened yet. After realizing we had been in an accident, I raised up, looked to my left, and saw Stewart. He was so quiet. Thinking he was passed out from the impact; I began searching for my phone. I looked out my window and saw a lady running towards me from the other side of the median. She tapped the window and pulled on the handle trying to help me. I yelled to help Stewart instead and I pushed to try and open the door, but I had no strength. She finally yanked it open and I breathed. I started screaming to help him; however, after walking over to him she quickly came back to me and said, "Let me help you." At this point, I am talking to Stewart, reassuring him that help was on the way and he would be ok. I felt his blood dripping on my arms, and it was warm. I thought everything would soon be okay.

A few minutes after calling my mom, the ambulance showed up. Eager to get Stewart help, I pleaded with them to not take me. I wanted to stick with him until his eyes opened. They were so damn adamant about keeping me calm and saying that they would get him next, forcing me onto the gurney. I was in so much pain and I could not walk. I was beginning to get hysterical because they wouldn't leave me alone, that they restrained me and put an oxygen mask on my face. After what seemed like forever, we arrived at the Med. While they rolled me back, I began to see familiar faces. Upon turning the corner to the examination room and seeing my mom and grandma, I immediately began to cry. I felt every touch and needle inserted into my body. I thought, "Enough of this mess. Where is Stewart?" All I wanted to do was hold him and cuddle under him.

Once they put me in a room, I kept asking the nurse where Stewart was, but no one knew. One nurse assured me that he was okay, and they would find out where he was. My dad then walked into the room where my family was with me and told me that Stewart had died at the scene. I screamed as loud as my body would allow me to, and they had to push me further down the hall because I was so loud. My soulmate was gone! We were so happy. Why would God allow this to happen to us at such a young age?

He was only 25 years old and I was 28. Our lives were just beginning to take off. It felt like everything in me broke that day. Me being accustomed to writing my feelings all the time was the only thing I had for release. I rarely expressed my feelings where others could see. No one around me could understand or fathom my pain. A widow at 28! This was absolutely unheard of. I was so angry at God, I never wanted to step into another church ever again.

People came by, called, sent letters, gave encouraging words, and prayed over and for me. I was secretly bitter that my friends and parents still had their spouses. Even the guy who hit us in the accident sent me a handwritten letter which only made me cry harder and get madder. He literally walked away from it while my husband died. The guy apologized in the letter, telling me about his family, telling me how the accident affected his life and how he put a memorial flower on the highway in remembrance of what happened. I appreciated the gesture and felt his sincerity, but it didn't help my heart and soul. No one could fully grip the amount of anger, hurt, pain, betrayal, loneliness, frustration, devastation, and disappointment that I was feeling. I didn't know how to grieve or cope with a loss so close to me. I felt so lost. I became even more introverted. I didn't want to talk about my feelings. I would write instead and at this point, I was journaling a few times a day. I slept a lot and lost weight. I smiled when other people were around me and cried when they weren't. I always wanted to be alone. Sometimes my friends would invite me to do things and if I knew their spouses were coming, I would quickly decline. I didn't want to be around love or see someone happily married. I was so broken inside.

♥

How could this have happened? Why was our relationship over so fast? Why was his life taken at such a tender age? Why this way? He had so much potential for being greater than what he already was. Matter of fact, he was up for pastoring at a church in the city at the time of the accident and it was leaning in his direction. He would have been ecstatic about pastoring again, and this church seemed very organized and eager for a new beginning.

His funeral was a week later on the 8th and I was dreading it. It had been such a stressful and heartbreaking week. His family was the worst. I mentioned before how they had personal issues with me. Well, that came out even more when he died. He was not close to his siblings or parents at the time of his death or half the time we dated. I knew there were strained relationships, and perhaps it drove them crazy that they would never get the chance to rectify their wrongs. It's a cliché but it's so true how you can tell how close families were when a person dies. They are usually the ones to make fools of themselves, express guilt which transforms into anger and hostility, and be completely irrational.

Once I gained strength to start planning his funeral, my dad and I invited his family over to discuss details. That was a complete mistake. They came over with such bad intentions and it showed as soon as they got out of the car. His family tried to fight everything I was planning to do for the service. They wanted me to wait on his childhood pastor to come back to the country, they wanted it at their home church, they wanted several things on the program, etc. His sister even called me a bitch, saying that he never loved me. Before I knew it, I was cursing her back out while trying to get up with my one good foot to slap the crap out of her. My best friend, Sydrea, was there trying to fight with me and she was nine months pregnant. It was such a scene, but thankfully my dad was there, and he kicked her out the house. He then took over saying everybody had things to say but nobody was offering help. They didn't pay for anything.

He let it be known to them all that I was the wife and whatever I said, stood. My parents paid for everything and for that I was grateful. We rarely saw eye to eye (and Lord knows we had issues) but when it really counted, they definitely showed up for me. Them being there for me during this time helped me see how much they cherished me and my life. It allowed me to let down my guard with them when expressing gratitude and the things that I needed during that time. Their support and love showed me that they genuinely cared for me and that they even wanted to be there for me. It truly meant a lot to me.

After everything Stewart's family did, I agreed to let the wake be at his home church. And guess what? They tried to get physical with my father, uncle, and other relatives there! Guilt and stupidity were running rampant throughout his family and I was sick of it. Now, I couldn't wait for the funeral because it meant I would be rid of them all. There were so many altercations surrounding the planning and wake that there were people on my behalf who were strapped at the funeral. Those who mattered knew what I had been dealing with concerning his family and they were prepared, including my dad, who was sitting in the pulpit with his peacemaker.

After the funeral, my dad decided to take me away for a while to regroup and then go back to church for the repast. I couldn't even go to my husband's burial. That was devastating, but I wanted to keep the peace and we knew that it would be horrible if we went. Other family members went, and my grandad did the burial. I cried; I couldn't even say a last "I Love You" to him. Not one time did it cross my mind that I wouldn't be able to be by his side all the way to the end. Me not being able to see him go into the ground was heart-wrenching. Even though I understood my dad wanting to keep me safe and avoid any further issues and unnecessary drama, it still hurt to not be able to say goodbye. I later found out that having that closure was necessary for my healing, and I wasn't able to have that.

Weeks later, his mom and I got him a headstone, together. I went to visit his gravesite a few times after the burial to get some me time, to say my goodbye's, and talk. It was refreshing to be able to have conversations with him. I felt relieved and that a small burden was lifted. After a few months, I couldn't go anymore. Emotionally, it kept taking a toll on me every time I went. I knew I needed to move forward and accept that he wasn't coming back to me. So, I resorted to writing out letters to him to get thoughts off my chest, sometimes even openly talking in an empty room as if he was there. Right after he passed, I went to Build-A-Bear and made a bear in his honor. I dressed him with a shirt, khakis, and a tie. He had a tool belt around his waist to symbolize Stewart's handiness, and he held a microphone in his hand to symbolize Stewart's preaching and singing. Stuffed in the bear's body were our wedding rings and his last sermon's manuscript. I slept with that bear for months.

♥

I knew that grief counseling would be something I needed, so I looked up a few places. They held a class at a church in Bartlett and I went; but after one session, I stopped going. I wasn't feeling it at all. I withdrew from family and friends. I don't remember how or when, but I came upon a verse in Psalms, 61:1-3. It read, "Hear my cry, O God; attend unto my prayer. From the end of the earth will I cry unto thee, when my heart is overwhelmed: lead me to the rock that is higher than I. For thou hast been a shelter for me, and a strong tower from the enemy" (King James Version).

Those three scriptures helped on numerous occasions. I personally challenge anyone to find a favorite verse, memorize it, and shout it out when you are feeling overwhelmed, alone, powerless, unmotivated, hurt, downtrodden, sad, anxious, depressed, and forgotten. Despite my anger and the above emotions, my foundation would not let me fall far. My Christianity still stood and, underneath it all, I knew that God was still there whether I wanted to receive or accept it.

"Safe in His Arms" by Rev. Milton Brunson and the Thompson Community Singers had become my source of strength. I listened to this song every day for reassurance that I was safe and still loved and protected. Even though I was still grieving, still hurt, still broken-hearted, still angry, buried underneath all this pain, I still had the knowledge that God had kept me safe. Before the collision, I remember sitting upright in the car, watching Golden Girls, and talking to Stewart. When I awakened after being blacked-out, I was laying down into the backseat of my car. My seat had been reclined. He kept me! He hid me! I still had a purpose to fulfill.

I still cry to this day whenever I hear that song.

I never expected to be a widow at such a young age. But, no one knows the plans for their life except God. Losing Stewart in such a drastic way was extremely painful, and God sparing my life in the process caused me extreme confusion. One of the questions I asked many nights was "Why me?" I had no idea as to why I was left to live, why I was left to grieve for my soulmate, why I didn't die, why the driver of the truck was speeding. I came to an understanding about not having all the answers. I would stress myself out even more trying to figure God out.

After everything had calmed down from the funeral and I had breathing time, my mom suggested a sabbatical to Nashville to have a girl's moment for me. I was so touched. It was A class all the way; I had my mom, grandma, godmother, two of my aunts, my sister, and my best friends with me. Sydrea couldn't make it because she had just delivered Adrian, my first godson. We took a limo there from Memphis and everything was great. There was prayer, meditation moments, clarity moments, supportive talks, and shopping. It was exactly what I needed during that time.

On the way back, we were discussing one of my favorite hobbies, reading. At one point, a suggestion was made to start a book club in Stewart's honor. It was one of my favorite things to do, a way to have fellowship and spend time with my friends, and it was symbolic because it was in his remembrance. I was pushed into being the president because of my organization skills and intolerance for excuses and noncommitment. It was such a great idea and I was so honored. We held our first meeting in October 2009, and we named it The Misfits Book Club.

♥

For the remainder of 2009 and the first half of 2010, I was on a downward spiral. No one quite knew because I didn't show it. I had started back going to counseling two weeks after the funeral and it was doing some good. I tried somewhere different this time, so I was learning about the steps of grief and how to begin coping. Suicidal thoughts were coming more and more, and my flesh was getting weak. I was having nightmares, seeing Stewart in my sleep, battling depression symptoms, and going through counseling for PTSD.

I continued to harbor a plethora of emotions. I tried to move forward. I started getting out of the house, attempting to be more social, singing in the choir at church, reaching out to people, but my mind and heart wouldn't let me be successful in doing so. My grief was still consuming me. I had become a functioning disaster!

I felt like I was losing my sanity; I was so alone and still so confused. I didn't understand how to function properly being a widow. I started jumping from guy to guy, only for pleasure. However, in the summer of 2010, I got into a relationship with Terrell. I was yearning to feel a connection with one person again. I was tired of random pleasure. We had developed a close bond by this point, so attempting to take it to the next level seemed right. He was so understanding, sweet, a musician, gave the best foot massages, and he was good in bed. I used to go support him whenever he had a gig and man, was it a turn on. We spent so much time together and we shared so many secrets and experiences. I loved him and he loved me. I shared deep feelings with him about Stewart and how I was grieving. He was so encouraging and wanted to be with me every step of the way for my healing. He started consuming my thoughts; I wanted to be around him all the time. He always cared about how I felt, and he was always there when he was needed and even when he wasn't. Our bond was so deep, he could always read between my words and sense through my tone that something was wrong and/or I wasn't being honest about my feelings.

However, I was afraid to totally love him, and I shared those emotions. We took everything a day at a time, so I felt no pressure. It felt so good to be cared about again. Even though I had feelings for him, I still wanted to be single. Isn't that crazy? I met other men before we became officially exclusive. And even after we broke up later that year, he still cared enough to check on me and not lose contact. During one of our off seasons, I started talking to this guy named John. During a visit to his house, I was sexually assaulted. Distraught and confused, I went home, cried, and fell asleep. The next day I called Terrell crying and told him what happened. He confirmed what I felt, I had been raped. He came over immediately and held me. I was so hurt, confused, and embarrassed. There was no love lost, and we picked back up on our relationship for about another year before it seriously ended. This relationship taught me how to own up to my truth. Terrell taught me how to be more vocal and how it is okay to not be okay. He forced me to talk out feelings instead of suppressing them. I definitely believed that I jumped into a relationship too soon after Stewart because I was still dealing with so much.

The best thing about our bond was that we started out as friends. Having that foundation between us made the relationship strong. We had so many good times and so many arguments. He reminded me of Stewart in a few ways, and sometimes that was an issue for me. He had his stubborn ways, and sometimes he would make me feel like he was a know-it-all. One thing that I always admired was his ability to tap into the Spirit. He prayed for me so many days and nights. I was an emotional wreck, going through depressive states and having so many triggers that I was so unaware of. I was up and down; I didn't know which way I was going.

As stated earlier, I decided to go to grief counseling, but didn't really do well with it; I tried and then completely gave up on it. I was just over talking about my feelings. I no longer wanted to dig deep. I was emotionally and mentally exhausted from thinking and crying. I just wanted to be. One thing grief counseling taught me was about the stages of grief. There are five: denial, anger, bargaining, depression, and acceptance. I learned after going through them that those stages are true and necessary to go through. There is no time limit on each step, so one could last months or even years. The key is to not remain in a stage for too long. That's another reason why support is crucial for anyone dealing with grief. It is too serious to go through it alone.

Anniversaries and birthdays began to roll around and I began to learn about triggers. Me riding in a vehicle with other people became such a stressor that every time I got in the car with someone new, I had to give them a pep talk on how to drive me around. I was a nervous wreck, and every little thing concerning an automobile frightened me. It was then I realized that I now knew firsthand what experiencing PTSD felt like.

♥

Scars. I have so many scars. I still remember the nurses pulling glass out of my skin and popping my toe back into place from it being dislocated. A week after the accident, in preparation for the funeral, my best friend Sydrea came over to do my hair. Glass was still embedded in it, and as she was shampooing and taking out glass, I cried. A year later, I had a constant pressure in my forearm and wondered what it was but could never see it. One day, the pain became unbearable and I pressed on my skin and felt something sharp. So, I cut my skin open and pushed until a triangular-shaped piece of glass came out. I cried in remembrance of where it came from.

I see scars from this accident every day. From a long gash on one arm, to several scar tissues from pieces of glass on the other arm, to the gash on my right toe from dislocation. Not only are my scars physical, but they are emotional, mental, and spiritual. I've been reminded every day since September 2, 2009 of what happened to me, what was taken from me, the pain I endured, and the loss of Stewart's life. In a sense, it makes me feel stronger to rub on my skin. While on the other hand, pain and hurt still sit with me.

This year makes 11 years since the accident, and it still pulls strong emotions out of me. Recurring dates that were important to us like birthdays or anniversaries don't bother me as bad anymore. However, when September 2nd rolls around each year, it feels like my heart knows before my mind what the date is. I wake up feeling sad, emotional, and moody. That rarely ever happens to me so when it does, I look at the calendar and it has always been the date of the accident. In the earlier years, if I was involved with someone when that time came around, I would feel so guilty. Then I had to deal with myself and reassure myself that it was okay to have moved on. To this day, riding with people, suddenly braking, dodging accidents, and seeing other car accidents around me makes me queasy inside. I cry, tense up, shake, zone out, etc. Grief is a process; it does not go away when you think it should, but it gets easier to cope with over time.

# KJ

The feeling of loneliness and being alone was beginning to surface in a powerful way. I wanted companionship. I honestly didn't care about pursuing anything long-term at the moment; I just wanted to feel like a woman and be loved again. Selfish? It was and I did not care. I hurt people during this time which I later regretted, but I only had so much to give. I didn't have much to offer but temporary pleasure and some conversation. I didn't want to give because I didn't want to feel.

December 2011, I met KJ at my job, Bank of America. We had seen each other quite often because he came in to do business for his employer. I never really gave him a second glance. I just did my job and was cordial as usual. However, one day in a small conversation, he asked me for my Facebook information. I gave it to him, and we began to conversate through Messenger which later turned into exchanging telephone numbers. We eventually began to hang out and it started becoming more and more frequent. I allowed myself the chance to be cared about once again but, to be honest, I know I didn't reciprocate much. I would try to show appreciation for the things he did, but I know that it wasn't my best effort. He showed me love and concern, and I was open to showing the same, it just wasn't at a healthy pace. I allowed him to do a lot while I did the minimum. I won't lie, I had my moments of thankfulness and showing that he mattered. They just weren't as frequent as his or I'm sure as much as he'd hoped. He was such a gentleman while we dated. He opened doors, initiated activities, bought me little gifts, loved to cuddle; it was nice to be admired again.

We went on trips, spent time together, and had fun. He took me on my first trip to New Orleans, he showed me places from his childhood, and we had a great time. We developed a good friendship which, in turn, became a relationship. It felt good to have something solid, a man who treated me like a princess and seemed to have his personal affairs in order. I started bringing him around family and friends and they all liked him. It was refreshing that I was in the state of mind to bring someone around my family, letting him into my world while also letting them into my world with him. Everyone loved his accent, me included, and he was so good with my godchildren.

After seven months of dating, he proposed. Underneath all the layers, my gut was urging me to say no; I wasn't mentally ready for something as definite as marriage again. But my mind and emotions wouldn't let me and, before I knew it, I had said yes. I was so excited about the idea of familiarity but terrified to be someone else's wife again. We set the date for seven months later, February 2013. I would be 31, the day before I turned 32. I consistently had doubts about everything, but no one knew because I kept them to myself. I figured I was just nervous and that it would pass. In hindsight, I later learned that it is always best to listen to yourself. It's also best to pray for confirmation before making drastic decisions such as intertwining your life with someone else's.

The wedding was beautiful. With Nick, I didn't have a lot of control over decorations, my sister Tracy and Sydrea were the only two in my wedding party, and it was planned pretty quickly. With Stewart, it was small and intimate, no wedding party, just me and him with my grandfather at the altar. We had close friends and family there, probably about 15 people total, but it was nothing formal. This wedding was everything I wanted from my dress, the bridal party, the attire and colors, the theme, to my wedding ring.

Had I backed out of this wedding; I would have let so many people down. Crazy huh? Putting others before myself and caring about what people thought versus what I needed to do, later came around and bit me like a mosquito bite on the ankle. The night of the wedding, I felt emotionally detached; we didn't even have sex that night. Who doesn't want or expect that? Despite the romance he provided and the gift of jewelry he gave on our wedding night, I still didn't feel it or him. Damn, I should have listened to myself months ago. I figured I was in this now, so I had to fight myself internally to make it work. Too much had been done at this point.

♥

He knew about Stewart and everything that our relationship consisted of, including his death. KJ also knew that I still had several emotional issues lingering. He told me that he wanted to be there for me, but it was becoming too hard for me to deal with it all: handling grief, learning to be a wife again, and needing to be there for him in every way possible. I can now admit that the marriage was very much one-sided. I was realizing that I didn't want to be anyone else's wife because I still desired Stewart. I still hadn't fully accepted that he was gone and could not come back to me. My heart was still in pieces, and I was not capable of moving forward on my own.

I truly cared for KJ, but love? I was not completely sold on it. He was a good man in the overall scheme of things, but aside from my own issues, he made me question his initial ability to be honest about his circumstances when we met. There were things I found out and had to call him out on throughout the relationship that caused me to question his capability of being a provider for the house. He wasn't as good with money as I thought, and he would make decisions and not tell me about them. Some decisions were made before me, but I was in the dark about them until they came to light. My sense of emotion was so lost that I didn't care about too much anymore. I had missed the idea of being married and loving someone else unconditionally. My vessel was so empty that nothing of substance poured out.

It was beginning to sink in that I needed to talk to someone again. But this time, I needed to find someone with credentials and a more solid background in their field of expertise. After researching for one, I found a psychiatrist and, within a few visits, I was diagnosed with depression. I was shocked and cried so hard, but it also explained so many things. I had always felt I had symptoms of something being wrong, but I never sought help for it. I was prescribed Cymbalta and instructed to start taking it daily. That day I contacted my sister Tracy for emotional backing, and she offered to go with me to tell my parents the news and have a discussion of support and next steps. Her offering to be there with me meant everything because we had not always been close growing up. I longed for a relationship with her, but we seemed to always butt heads. It felt good to be able to reach out to her for help and sisterly love and it actually be given on her behalf. However, when we made it to my parents' house and shared what was told to me, I was completely let down. The conversation was the total opposite of encouragement and support. I was literally told to "not have a pity party" and that "we are going to just pray about it." This reaction caused an instant withdrawal from me and my parents once again.

I cried so hard at the term "pity party" being used. Depression is a real thing and, even at that time when mental health wasn't such a priority or common topic, I knew that it was a serious issue. To not be shown support from my own parents was heartbreaking, and once again my vulnerability was rejected by the people it should have mattered the most to. They knew I was still dealing with grief, how many days I couldn't sleep, how I called for prayer from my uncle and cousin in the middle of the night, how my current marriage was on the rocks, how I had basically secluded myself from a lot of social activity. Yet, not one red flag was seen. Moreover, "Let's pray about it" and "Don't have a pity party" was the only response. Me being medically diagnosed and put on meds to help ease my pain, anxiety, and to help me focus was not enough! I was tired and exhausted.

I had tried to let them in, and I was shut down. I wanted to die. Suicidal thoughts were brimming again. I tried to push them away. I suppressed them as much as I could. This is when bad personal habits began to form. I was drinking way more and even started smoking clove cigars. They helped me ease my mind when I needed to escape and just breathe.

♥

The bright side to 2013 was my sister getting pregnant; it was such a bright moment and time in my life. I made myself available for every aspect and detail of her pregnancy. As I mentioned earlier, we never had a sisterly relationship and I always wanted to change our relationship for the better, but I never knew how to successfully do so. This baby was our glue and I saw it, so I used it as the olive branch to strengthen what we had. I wanted to do everything with her and for her. This baby would not only be an addition to the family, but he was strengthening what was already there. I was excited for what was to come.

KJ and I were still having difficulties and I was feeling overwhelmed and needed space. I offered to move in with Tracy to help her around the house and do whatever needed to be done to help with the coming of my nephew. Cleaning up, cooking, being a chauffeur, going to all her appointments, anything that was needed.

Once Hazen was born that October, I knew I had to live for him. I felt God was giving me a new chance to love someone unconditionally. I said it then and I still say it now, Hazen was my saving grace and I will never forget it! He means so much to me for so many reasons and I will always be appreciative!

I had a newfound strength and I focused on my truth. I moved back home that November to try and work things out with my husband. I was struggling at this point because my marriage was on the rocks, and I had been questioning myself about remaining at my church home. I was not feeling satisfied sexually, and mentally I wasn't really available. I was taking Cymbalta, so my moods were pretty mellow but, after some time passed, I took myself off of the pills. KJ and I were not on the same page when it came to emotions; he wanted more, and I felt I was pushing to show what I could. I was still conversing with people from my past and even started talking to someone new to try and fill the voids.

♥

I was beginning to feel stagnant in every aspect of my life. January 12, 2014, my grandad preached a sermon titled

"Go Back and Try Again". This struck a chord in me because I was ready to quit everything. I listened intently and took every word to heart. In the sermon, he touched on church, remaining faithful/dedicated, and trying to make things work in a marriage.

After church that day, KJ and I went out to eat and discussed the sermon and how our relationship was going. I asked him about his thoughts on open marriages. To my surprise, he wasn't against it. We discussed possible what-ifs and left the conversation open with no decision. We talked about it again the next day, along with our current state in the marriage and even divorce.

After that conversation, we continued to try until I couldn't anymore. I filed for divorce in February 2014. When I moved back to my home with him, we tried to make up for lost time and to make things right. It was not working, at least for me. I no longer wanted to focus on the marriage because I felt trapped emotionally and mentally. I needed to get over Stewart. It was weird because when KJ and I dated, we were fantastic. But as soon as I said, "I Do," a switch flipped, and my heart froze.

He was a good man and he deserved more than what I gave. It took me a minute, even while separated, to understand that until I dealt with me, I would continue hurting people. It was critical that I got back to me. I needed to discover who I was and pray for purpose. I needed to heal.

KJ and I had a great courtship and the marriage had some good points, but I consistently leaned upon my own understanding and not God's. I couldn't see any other way to make it better except to divorce. I no longer wanted him to lack what he needed as a man and a spouse. I was in no shape to give and, even though he wanted to help me through it all, I let him go. I felt it was the unselfish thing to do. My intent was for his happiness, or so I thought. I guess I still didn't fully take hold of the part in the vows about "for better or worse." I should have at least allowed him to be there for me, and we could have worked on reestablishing us at the same time. That choice I did grow to regret, but it taught me a lot at the same time.

# CHANGE OF SCENERY: HOUSTON

After filing for divorce for the second time, I was at peace for trying to do things just for me. I realized that I had never solely been independent, and that needed to change. After visiting my brother in Houston that May of 2014, my father suggested moving there to gain a fresh start on life. Never wanting to be somewhere as big as Houston, I pushed it to the back of my mind. After diligently seeking for employment to function as I needed to as an adult, it was becoming frustrating because I was getting no hits from employers. I started to reconsider my dad's suggestion on starting over somewhere new. I had no attachments; I was going through a divorce and had no kids. I decided to talk to my brother and get his advice on moving, starting over, and new opportunities.

KJ and I were still living together even though we were separated. It was weird because I was doing my own thing and so was he. Once I made the decision to move, I discussed details with him and offered to let him stay in my house if he paid the bills. The day after my court hearing for the final judgment of divorce on July 24, 2014, I was on the road to Houston with a packed car of my personal belongings. This move had so many meanings behind it. This would be the time for rebuilding, discovering who I was, what I wanted, and embracing new adventures. I made a vow to continue my education and finish my courses for my bachelor's degree. I was already enrolled in my first set of classes before I touched Texas soil. Despite the excitement of moving, I was still sad and had several moments of self-doubt and anxiety about the what-ifs. I was leaving everything and everyone I knew. Could I really do this? Did I really know how to be independent? What if I failed? Did I make the right decision?

It was always my understanding that God had a way of making life uncomfortable to help bring out the best in a person; however, a person has to willingly submit to the journey and stay the course. I was so afraid of getting on the road, I cried pulling out of my driveway. Not for my ex, but because I had never made such a big decision in my entire life. Moving to Chicago was big, but I was with someone else and very rebellious. I didn't really care back then. This time was different. There were so many uncertainties. I had to rely on God for this move.

♥

I arrived in Houston on July 25, 2014 with no job lined up, and I quickly learned that it was not about what I knew but who I knew. There were a lot of frustrating days and nights, and I slipped into depressive states quite often from the letdowns of employment, friends, and men. Friends were nonexistent upon moving there, but I did develop a friendship with a few people that eventually turned sour. Men were such a joke. Because I was new there, I relied on dating sites to meet people. And the people I met turned out to be habitual liars. They posted great things about expectations and goals, but once I met them or talked to them, I found out that they were only searching for sex partners. It began to get old, so I just began deleting apps and numbers out of my phone.

Thinking back on when I finally made the decision to move to Houston, I knew I had to be mentally prepared for being somewhat on my own. My brother was already there, so I knew I wasn't totally alone, but I had to be able to vouch and provide for myself. On the road, I was confident in finding a great job, confident in regaining my self-confidence, confident in finally finishing school and graduating with my bachelor's degree. I had such high hopes for this new phase of my life, and I was determined to not give up when hard times showed up. After a short while, I began to work one to two jobs at a time, while remaining in school full-time. I was slowly finding my way career-wise, but my personal life was a total disaster. I wasn't really the social butterfly like people may expect moving into a city as big as Houston. I had never been an outgoing person. If a person wanted to say something, they had to come to me. I was always locked in my room when I was young (my choice, I guess) so I grew into being by myself: just me, my notebook, and my music. I never liked large crowds, so I was never into going to clubs or large parties. Being around family and close friends was the most that I would do, and I enjoyed it. I also enjoyed hurrying back home so I could be by myself.

On those dating apps, I ran across so many grown little boys it wasn't funny. I was exhausted and consistently hurt from the constant letdown that I was on the verge of completely shutting down from men altogether. I had even jokingly said that I would only date girls because men were too stressful and childish. Over time, this was a huge contemplation. Emotionally, I was checked out, and my mind and heart were trailing closely behind.

In October of 2016, I joined Lily Grove, a church that reminded me of home. Very traditional teachings, and the pastor knew how to stir up the emotions if you know what I mean. Needless to say, I was comfortable, but my growth was very stagnant. I wasn't active at all, only a pew member whenever I decided to go. Ever since the car accident in 2009, my faith remained tarnished; I even began to wonder if it still existed. My foundational teachings from childhood about church were important. We were at every service and every event. It was a habit. We were forced to be at church every waking moment that it was open. The problem was, building my own personal relationship with God and everything that came with doing so was never significantly pointed out. I had been using, borrowing, feeding off my parents, grandparents, and my best friends' spiritual relationships for so long that I was spiritually lost.

I was empty......

# CHARLIE

In December of 2016, I met Charlie on Tinder. I had previously met several guys on there, but they were all full of crap. Either they were there for a one-night stand or to take advantage of someone and waste their time. This was my second time reactivating my account when I swiped across Charlie's picture and profile. We chatted there for a little while then we agreed to meet in person. It was a flop because he left his wallet at home and didn't realize it until he made it to our meeting destination. I was turned off in a way, so we stood outside and talked for a second then we parted ways. We talked the next day, and from there we were always on the phone and spending time together.

At the time, I was living with a friend and her kids until I could get back on my feet. Previously, I had been living with an ex-boyfriend who didn't know how to be honest about not wanting to be in a relationship anymore. I was so frustrated and unhappy with the entire situation that I had contemplated moving back home to Tennessee several times. After numerous conversations, Charlie offered me a key to his apartment as a place of refuge and peace when I became overwhelmed. I was so grateful for that offering and I took him up on it. I was so happy that I could finally be comfortable being an introvert in peace. During these months, I was working and completing my last few months of undergrad. This had been a long time coming! I had started and quit school for over two years. Getting my degree was one of my top goals when I moved to Houston. I was excelling too; I was on the Dean's List, had been inducted into the Alpha Sigma Lambda Honor Society, maintained a

3.8 GPA all three years, and already been given the congrats for graduating Magna Cum Laude! The end of school was so close. Externally I appeared to be happy and excited, but, internally, I was miserable and unhappy with myself.

One day (Jan. 5, 2017) while writing in my journal, I wrote an entry titled "Failure". Here's what it said:

> Failure is what I feel like…I don't know what I'm doing wrong or even doing right at this point...SMH…I've applied to numerous jobs nonstop while employed and even unemployed and nothing has come through!! It is now 2017 and I'm still unemployed and feeling worse than ever. It is so hard masking my true feelings of wanting to break down and scream!! I apply, I follow up, I pray, I remain consistent, I do my best to keep positive…. What more is there?!?!? Everyone around me (meaning my siblings) are constantly being blessed and elevated in their career. And me, the oldest, is still in the same predicament. It's depressing…I'm so drained…I am about to be 36 in a month and what do I have to show for it? I live with my best friend and her children and do substitute teaching, which means I wait for someone else to not go to work for me to work… How is that living?? I'm at my wits' end. I don't know what else to do…

I was in a desperate place. I was feeling less than a woman, I had endured so much hell for so long that I was mentally exhausted and emotionally fed-up. I felt as if I deserved so much more from God at this point in my life. Hadn't I been through enough?!

♥

April 2017, I moved in with Charlie. It was cool in the beginning, but there was this underlying pit of the stomach feeling that I could not shake. I kept ignoring it. After about a month or two, he started to change from the person I met, religiously. He started listening to this online pastor on YouTube and it started to become annoying to me. Not because he was trying to better himself, but because I was feeling forced to hear it and I didn't want to. I was annoyed at times because there were always references made to the preacher whenever we had a serious conversation. At times, I felt he was beginning to worship this man's every word because he talked about him so often. I enjoy conversations, and I love asking questions to gain insight on things. However, I don't like feeling like someone's opinion is being forced on me, nor do I like when it feels like a person can't think for themselves. Now Charlie was (and is) a very intelligent person, which was one of the characteristics that I was attracted to when we first met. But this newfound preacher had begun to take a toll on me to the point that I began tuning out whenever I heard his name. Certain things about Charlie began to change, and then the conversation of us shacking up began to surface.

Now, being the preacher's kid that I am, I knew shacking up before marriage was wrong, but at this point I was comfortable. Getting married was becoming a conversation more than I wanted it to. These were the prime moments to be truthful to him and open up about my insecurities and feelings, but I chose to not be completely honest. I was too afraid to be vulnerable. I was afraid that I would say the wrong thing, hurt his feelings, make the wrong choice, or not be taken seriously for feeling the way I felt. In my past, being vulnerable and expressive got me nowhere, I didn't know how to truly be honest with my heartfelt feelings. There was no real proposal, but I did later find out that he had reached out to my dad to talk to him and ask for my hand in marriage. That gesture made me feel like a little girl. It made me feel honored and worthy of having his last name. It made me feel loved.

♥

I had a vacation to California coming up the first of September, but because of Hurricane Harvey hitting Houston late that August, I had to reschedule it for the end of the month. Charlie suggested that we get married while we were there and, against my better judgment, I agreed. So, on September 26th, at the age of 36, I was another man's wife, again. The wedding ceremony was absolutely beautiful, and I couldn't have asked for a better atmosphere. We got married on the beach in Coronado. Charlie, his mother, grandmother, and other family friends planned and prepared everything. He had made my ultimate dream wedding of marrying on the water come true! How could I tell him I was having second thoughts?

The second thoughts began once I got on the plane to leave Houston. So many thoughts were rushing forward. Are you sure? Do you really love him or is this a strong like? If he annoys you so much, why did you say yes? Is he really the one? Are you attracted to him? I kept battling myself with answers and attempted to look at the bigger picture. I did feel he was good for me and my future because of how he thought ahead. Would that be enough? I made myself think it was enough because I went through with everything. I had never had someone take charge of my dream and make it a reality; it was my fantasy wedding. No one in my family made the wedding, mainly because everything was planned so quickly. My friend at the time came and that was enough for me.

No one had a negative thing to say regarding the marriage. If they did, they never said it to me. I did get questioned by those who knew about my history, but that was it. Once again, I suppressed my truth.

♥

When we arrived back to Houston as husband and wife, it still felt the same as before we left unmarried. I was emotionally detached, spiritually shut down, and physically turned off. We had always been friends. Shouldn't our bond be better now that we were married? What the hell is wrong with me? I asked myself this question almost on a daily basis. There was no emotional connection, and a lot of nights we went to bed upset. I later figured out that he was not the best with managing money and loved to play tit for tat. Not being able to manage his money, take me out, or buy me gifts was a huge turn off and something that I never wanted to deal with again. My last two husbands before him, Stewart and KJ, were terrible at managing money and paying bills. After Stewart, I was adamant about paying bills, on time, myself. No one ever carried my weight, but it seemed like I was having to help with everyone else's. I was starting to see that here and I didn't like it. We rarely ever went out as a couple; and when we did, nine times out of ten, I would pay. His tit for tat petty ways were too much as well. Sometimes, I would laugh because I was simply not accustomed to a man being petty with me. Not only just a man, my husband.

He used to address the concern all the time about me not initiating sex. I explained to him that no one had ever complained before. Initiating was new to me; I had always been with men who simply took what they wanted. Now, I will say that I have initiated after being intoxicated to a certain extent. But that was with motivation of the drink; however, on my own and sober, I never did it, nor did I ever have a complaint about me not making the first move. I said that I would work on it time after time, but it never came. I began to wonder why it was so hard to show my need for him, to initiate what should be natural between a man and wife. I discovered that I simply didn't want to because there was no desire to do so.

After many weeks and months of conversations, arguments, and no intimacy, Charlie suggested I speak with someone regarding my lack of emotions. This was marriage number four and I did not want it to go down the drain, but I knew something was wrong. This time I wanted to do whatever it took to make it work before making a hasty and wrong decision.

I eventually took his advice and on May 2, 2018, I began my journey of digging deep into Takenya.

# THE QUEST

I went through two counselors to get to the charm of number three. The first one was so adamant about grief being my marital issue that it was the only focus of our sessions. She was so off course. The second counselor was a complete joke. She had her PhD, so I had such high expectations for her. I wanted to support black women professionals, so I looked one up online. She was an older lady and had several credentials behind her name. My initial session with her was a disaster. She would ask a question, I would answer, then she would stare. Ten minutes later, another question came, I answered, then she would stare. This repeated for the entire hour of the appointment. After two sessions, I was over it and never went back. Still determined and refusing to give up, I kept searching for what I needed. After the two failed attempts through assistance with my job's Employee Assistance Program (EAP), I sought someone entirely off their list. I located a therapist who had great credentials, so I called and made an appointment.

Within these few months of failed counsel, having sabbatical moments to myself, and talking to a few trusted family members, Charlie and I decided to separate inside the house. We lived like roommates; I slept and lived in the bedroom and he slept and lived up front in the living area. He understood what I needed to do for me, but he also wanted to be my support system throughout the process. I was very appreciative of his offer and concern. Divorce was discussed quite often, but we did not want to make any definite decisions, so we just agreed to separate.

August 7<sup>th</sup>, 2018, I had my first appointment with my new therapist. She was exactly what I needed! She was intuitive, a listener, and a digger. She asked questions and paid attention to every answer. She questioned my answers, which pulled out information that I didn't think was important. Going all the way back to my childhood was where my history of issues began. From there, the unhappiness, unworthiness, hatefulness, despitefulness, promiscuity, and rebellion roots were uncovered.

♥

The first issue uncovered was how I always felt like the black sheep of the family. I wasn't close to anyone in that house. My closest person was my best friend, Sydrea. We were eight months apart in age and basically grew up together. She knew everything about me. With my parents, I always got in trouble because of my rebellion, and I was never close with my sister and brother. I am four-to-five years apart from them both. They were like Frick and Frack, they were born a year apart. They did everything together. I played with them somewhat when we were small, but once boys came into the picture and I got my phone in my room, I was done. My sister used to snitch on me all the time, which I grew to despise as any older sibling would. Now, we had family trips and fun moments as a family, don't get me wrong. However, if you were to pick up a microscope and really look, a person would see so many cracks it would seem unreal. I never felt like I measured up to my siblings. I felt like they were loved more than me; to me, it was very visible.

Rules were bent, more money and/or help was given when needed, and they never got in trouble. My counselor asked me how the relationship was present day, and I told her it was better but not consistent. I still sometimes feel cast out by them and sometimes a little jealous. They are a year apart, so naturally they had a closer bond growing up. A huge portion of my teenage life I was more into boys than family. As an adult, I wanted to be close and form a relationship, but I felt the disinterest. Honestly, I felt like I was the baby instead of Tracy. Everything seemed so backwards. I had so many issues. I was unstable, financially messed up, and unaware of what I wanted out of life. Here I am, the oldest and the most screwed up!

They both had so many things going for them and I was just lost. My counselor helped me focus on the positives and pointed out that my path was not theirs. It was possible that my life was harder at home because I was the first, so it was like a crash course. By the time my parents got to my sister and brother, they knew what to do and not do. Hell, even my sister and brother knew what not to do because I was in trouble all the time. She helped me understand that it's not healthy to compare. Instead, I should use it as a source of motivation. I must make sure I'm doing my part to build a relationship with them. No, we don't talk every day, but I love them both to death. I had to give myself more credit and not make myself feel less important than they were.

♥

With more sessions to follow, more seeds to those roots were discovered in my relationship with my parents. From that discovery, I found that the issue had a specific name: VULNERABILITY. I didn't know how to be vulnerable to anyone I came close to or was intimate with, and we had to find out why. Of course, I wasn't born that way so an event or series of them had to trigger this dysfunction, right? RIGHT! In one session, I discussed with her when I felt the disconnect with my parents. That first event was when my diary was broken into.

Most girls remember when stores used to sell the little pretty diaries with the petite padlocks with small keys attached to them. Well, I had one that I used to write my most intimate thoughts in. My feelings, whether good or bad, and my experiences with boys were on every page. Yes, I had those because I was already having sex when I received my first diary. Hell, at the age of 12 I wasn't pure anymore. Was I ashamed? No! The reason being, I didn't feel noticed at home or appreciated; I had always felt like the outcast of the family. Do I think it was entirely intentional, of course not. But that did not diminish how I felt. There were so many freaking rules in that house that it was not funny. Everything was church related which I grew to despise. So, I started getting attention from boys and I liked it. A little too much. It was sort of my source of feeling complete, wanted, needed, worthy, beautiful, enough, and desired. Not realizing that my mind and body were continuously being damaged and destroyed, I did what felt good at the time.

On this particular day, I got home from school and my mom approached me with my diary in her hand. It was unlocked. She had broken into it and read all my secrets and most private thoughts. I was devastated and immediately began to detest her. My diary was my heart; it showed every part of me at its purest state. No one knew of my personal thoughts or feelings. I questioned a lot of things about myself on those pages, along with confessing to so many good feelings as well as bad. All my insecurities, wrongdoings, and explorations were there. I had watched enough *Cosby Show* episodes to know that conversations between parents and kids, mothers and daughters were essential. That's how many lessons were supposed to be learned and trust was gained. Why would a mother do this? What was wrong with actually talking and having a mom/daughter moment?

The disdain kicked in when I got a whooping and put on punishment for harboring feelings, acting out, and not feeling comfortable enough to voice my true feelings. There was no conversation as to what was seen and read. I was just directly disciplined with no question as to "why". That hurt. That created a huge wall within my body. I was immensely hurt to my core that I could get in trouble for something as honest as my thoughts. I was childishly expecting questions, sex conversations, loving banter, compassion, maybe even special attention because of the things I wrote. I got none of that.

♥

Another incident was when I was about 16 years old and I was taken to my family's OBGYN doctor after being caught with a boy hiding in the closet. I will never forget the doctor because she told my mom that not only was I sexually active, but I also had an STD. My mom was upset, which was expected, but the reaction to the news was the problem. I got slapped, whooped, and my bedroom was moved from upstairs to downstairs, right next to my parents. Was that a solution? Not at all! Once again, no conversation, no show of motherly concern to see or find out the cause for my actions. No birds and the bees conversation. Just disciplined. This is where my hardcore shell began to build its emotional structure.

Fast forward to twelfth grade during my senior trip, I was 18 years old. A few of my classmates and I were snitched on for having boys in our room. That resulted in getting suspended and a paddling. The suspension was for around three days if I remember correctly. I got home from school right as the office called the house and my dad was answering the telephone. I don't know what was said on that phone because, when he got off, there was no dialogue between the two of us. He told me to get a switch from a tree in the backyard. In that kitchen, I was whooped with a switch and the weight belt he used when he went to work out at the gym. I don't even classify it as a whooping—I was basically beaten that day. There was another moment that I will not expound upon at this time that made me very fearful. I could see the anger on his face, and I was terrified. My sister and brother were standing in the kitchen's doorway to the den crying and witnessing the entire thing. I was shattered and emotionally broken. I was so hurt mentally and physically that I could not move off the floor. I hated him that very day.

Where was the "Let's get to the bottom of this" dialogue? Where was the humanity? Where was the concern? I was severely broken in that instant. How could a father treat his own child, his daughter, that way? Was I that bad of a child? Why not ask me questions first? If I was such a rebellious and disobedient child, which I was, why not try to find out why? I had so many cry outs for help, and they were all ignored and addressed in an uncaring fashion.

Let us not forget that dreadful night in twelfth grade which I spoke of in the beginning, that helped shape my outlook on men period. My choices were taken away. I was with someone who I felt safe with, and he basically walked me into the wolves den. My feelings didn't count, my respect was nonexistent, my worth wasn't considered. It was impossible for me to not want to be with a man, but it was easy for me to not give all of me anymore. I taught myself how to not care after a certain extent.

I immediately became emotionally withdrawn more and more after each incident. Why should I show any form of emotion to anyone? Would it honestly matter? The people I thought were supposed to love me the most made me feel that being vulnerable and open was unnecessary. Every time I had a sensitive moment warranting conversation or concern, I was punished for it. In my eyes, I was treated and felt like a disgrace.

Uncovering the past with my therapist really hurt, and the disappointment felt awful, but it led me to my truth. I had unknowingly blocked myself at an early age from wanting to ever be vulnerable with another being, and it showed in every relationship I involved myself with.

♥

This had been my hindrance throughout all my serious relationships, my four marriages. I lived in fear of being my true authentic self, being free to love and be loved, to be accepted for my flaws and mistakes, to be free with my feelings and desires. This level of fear caused me to make several premature decisions, caused me to say yes when I really should have said "hell naw", caused me to stay in comfort when I should have left or never been involved from the beginning, caused me to put myself in uncompromising positions just so the other person wouldn't be disappointed in me, caused me to lie and say "I love you" when I should have said "I'm not ready" or "No, I'm not in love with you".

Within these several months of going through numerous therapy sessions, I was also reading Sarah Jakes Roberts' book, *Don't Settle for Safe*. It felt like I was reading about myself on every page. In the chapter of "Knowing Your

Roots", she spoke on the importance of knowing your DNA, mainly your parents and where they came from. So many gems throughout that chapter helped give me courage for the inevitable: "If those disconnects are never confronted and healed, then we become adults full of words we never said and emotions we never processed" (Jakes Roberts, 2017).

For me to get out of this world of unhealthy living, being emotionless, and reckless decision making I needed to fully confront the cause of it all. I had to have a sit-down, face-to-face, conversation with my parents.

# THE ROAD TO RECOVERY

Monday, the 12<sup>th</sup> of November, I was a nervous wreck. The day had come for the weighty conversation with my parents. I had previously informed my sister and brother about my plan, and they wanted to be there for support. This meant the world to me, especially because it wasn't mandatory. They wanted to be with me. I was so touched that they cared that much for me and my growth. They had witnessed so much of my lifelong ups and downs, and I was full of gratitude that they wanted to be a part of my healing journey. Charlie, despite our marriage being on the rocks, had already reassured me that he would be there. He told me that if no one was in my corner, he would stay in town to help see me through this pivotal point with his presence and support. My freedom depended on this moment. I was fed up with my past issues continuing to bombard my present and future. This was for my liberation, regardless of who was on board.

I already had about seven pages written out with everything that had been on my heart and buried in my mind since the age of twelve. We all met at my sister's house and, once everyone was settled, I began to read. My past hurt, my present hurt, and things that no one in that room knew I had harbored inside of my heart and soul. Once I finished reading and wiping my tearful eyes, I exhaled and immediately felt a huge weight lift from my entire body. I walked in that house with no expectation but with the confidence in knowing that, no matter the outcome, I would be speaking my truth and doing what was best and healthy for me.

Upon admission, they both wholeheartedly stated that I was the firstborn, and with that came a lot of uncertainty. They mostly parented according to what they saw their parents do and they sort of "winged" the rest of it. My mother did what she saw my grandmother do, which was mostly keep the house and remain silent. This showed why I never felt she spoke up for me. She also said she didn't have a lot of conversations with Granny, so maybe she didn't know how to confront or be honest and relate to her own daughter. My dad went through a childhood of a holy, churchgoing mother as well; however, my grandfather was abusive. He was also mistreated by his own sister, and he didn't properly approach or respond to females in the best way. Seeing violence and mistreatment to the woman who meant the most to him at that time (his mom) and having to defend himself is a lot to figure out and even learn from at a young age. Don't get me wrong, my parents are beautiful inside and out. Anyone that has ever encountered them could attest to that statement. My conflict was on the parenting and my non-existent relationship with them throughout my years at home.

Believe me when I say, this transparency is not for bashing anyone nor to make any individual feel bad. However, this is my truth, good or bad. I lived it, dealt with it, and grew from it. My hope is that other parents will understand and see through me the importance of talking to your kids. Let them know who you were and who you are. No one is perfect and no child expects perfection. On the flip side of that, children do expect love, tenderness, compassion, and simply feeling like their feelings matter. There were so many things I wished I did not learn from experience. I wish there had been lessons shared, open non-judgmental conversations had, and more one on one experiences.

Uncovering my issues and hearing them confess and come clean about theirs really showed my siblings and me a different side of them. By the time my siblings became of age, a lot of lessons were learned on what to do and not do. Despite the pain it inflicted on me, I understood their positions at the time and sincerely forgave them that very instant. I left my sister's house that night an emotional wreck, yet relieved and at ease. I also realized I had accomplished step one and was on my way to complete healing.

♥

Two days later, Charlie left for California and I had a hard decision ahead of me.

On my birthday in 2019, I made the decision to let it all go. I headed downtown and filed for divorce. This would make divorce number three. It was hard to do but, after being honest with myself, I did not want to make another mistake of staying around. I no longer wanted to live a lie. We never should have gotten married in the first place, and that was something we both agreed on. I had to do what was necessary. Despite my predicament of having four marriages before 40 (38 to be exact) I learned valuable lessons from each man.

# INFERTILITY

I was unsure about writing about this particular soft spot in my life because it always makes me cry. But this was another battle that I had to emotionally and mentally overcome, so it is only right that I include it.

Since the age of 11, I always wanted kids. It was not until my second marriage that I began to question my ability to have children. After Stewart died, I was actually happy that we didn't have kids because I never wanted to have kids as a single mother. Please, do not misunderstand me, there is nothing wrong with it, but that is not what I wanted for my life. The way our marriage ended would have been even harder if we had children together. Me seeing him in them daily and growing up without their father would have been way more complicated than it already was with just me to look after and grieve properly.

When I met KJ, the longing for children resurfaced again. I didn't voice my concerns until later, once we were married. I didn't feel comfortable talking about such a touchy subject while dating. So, I waited until I felt secure about him wanting children to open up about something I wanted so badly. After having an intimate conversation with him, I finally grew enough confidence to move forward. I researched and finally located a specialist to help me find the source of the issue and possibly rectify it. I'd had sex for so long and at this point had three husbands with no pregnancies. Something was wrong and it was time to find out what it was. I went to Fertility Associates of Memphis and became a patient of Dr. Ke. I loved him because he was so sweet and very understanding. He made sure I understood everything, and he was very thorough in uncovering the problem. After an extensive and painful test, he discovered that I had bilateral hydrosalpinx, blocked tubes. This was devastating because had it been only one tube, my possibilities would have been cut in half but still possible. Having both of my tubes blocked was a big blow. Me becoming pregnant was basically out the window. Without surgery, I could never physically have my own child. Another coal to the already burning fire.

♥

He did offer alternatives. He suggested having surgery: laparoscopy/hysteroscopy. This would be performed in hopes of two possible outcomes: fimbrioplasty, which would be to repair my tubes or neosalpingostomy, which would be to open the tubes. So, after many discussions with KJ and my mom, I made the appointment to have the operation done that December 2012.

Dr. Ke stated that there was a large amount of scarred tissue blockage, but he was successfully able to open my tubes and that I had a limited amount of time to try and conceive. I recovered well from the surgery and had sex once it was safe to try again. Needless to say, I did not get pregnant, and from follow up appointments, I was told my tubes had closed again. Another option was offered: insemination. This process was less invasive, and I had doubts but still wanted to do whatever I could. So, in 2013,

I had the procedure done. After that was a fail, he stated that my only other option would be in vitro fertilization (IVF).

After all these attempts, I began to become angry with myself, and quickly, the anger turned into depression. The main reason I blamed myself was because of the initial problem, my tubes being blocked. The take-home research from the doctor's office gave a definition of the probable cause, one factor, which was a pelvic infection is usually caused by sexually transmitted diseases. My mind wandered back to when my mom took me to the doctor at the age of 16, where I found out I had an STD. This particular day stood out because I had been having sex since the age of 12. For four years, I had both protected and unprotected sex. I could have had an infection unknowingly for years. I felt like I did it to myself; one of my biggest desires, I took it away from my own damn self. Because of longing to feel loved, wanted, and desired, I hurt myself in the long run.

I also felt like God punished me for damaging myself and being promiscuous so early in age. I felt like he took the one thing that I desired more than anything, kids. It took a long time before I was able to answer questions without getting mad, offended, or teary-eyed about why I did not have kids. I used to shut down or snap in response, but now I just say, "I was never blessed with them," or "When God is ready for me to have them, I will," and walk away. I had to heal from this pain, blame, and anger. It still bothers me to be honest, but it is no longer an uncomfortable strain. I know my options and I am at peace with them.

❤

The blessing in this was me being a godmother. It started with Kennedy in 2006, then Carter, Adrian, Sara, Ivy, Taylor, and Alex Jr. Oh, and not to mention I am an aunt to two boys, Hazen and soon to be Addison (July 2020). He will be a few months old by the time this book is released. I am still blessed. My best friends saw the best in me and asked me to be what I always wanted despite my circumstances. I will always love these kids like they are my own and treat them as such.

# MY COMEBACK

Healing is a MUST! There is no moving forward if you don't heal. I had made up in my mind at the start of my counseling sessions that I no longer wanted to be who I was anymore. I was ready for change. I wanted more, and deep down still desired a real true foundational love. I deserved it and I was willing to do everything in my power to make sure I got it. I am a survivor in so many ways, and I was no longer willing to let my past determine my destiny!

There is such a stigma against counselors, therapists, psychologists, life coaches, mentors, and others in the healing profession. Those people are essential. However, they are only as successful as the individual seeking their help. A person must be open-minded, open-hearted, open to digging deep, open to reopening wounds, dedicated, willing to embrace the tears and hurt, truthful, determined, and ready to grip whatever comes from the experience.

I can say with an honest heart that those four men simply loved me for who I was and cared for my well-being. A lot of people used to ask me what I did to get so many rings for marriage, and I answered, "I don't know" each time. I truly had no idea what led to each proposal, I only knew how to be me. Down-to-earth personality, positive attitude, responsible, loved to be at home, loved sex, fluffy body, easy to talk to, loved trying new things (including in bed), and catered to what they needed (mostly). All my serious relationships resulted in a proposal within months. None of them ever expected me to not be myself, except for Stewart, but that was handled.

However, the issue with each marriage was me. I was the common denominator in each equation, and until I realized I had an issue, I would have forever been that shared trait. Thankfully, I heard my last ex-husband's concerns and listened. Moreover, it was his unbiased and unselfish acts to be supportive that pushed me to seek the root of my dilemma. My actions had always been the same throughout each relationship, but the support, love, intuition, and honesty of him telling me what he saw made the difference.

God never makes mistakes. Common statement, but it is so true. Despite our marriage not lasting, Charlie's purpose to me was to open my eyes about myself, my relationship with my parents, and my relationship with God.

♥

On the last Sunday of 2018, I joined my current church, The Church Without Walls. That was my second goal to achieve after reaching my first goal of speaking with my parents. Without God, I am absolutely nothing! I had death at my door a few times in life and He kept me! I questioned what He allowed to happen to me, yet, He kept me! I lost faith and hope in Him for years, yet, He kept me!

I have been focused on me and my well-being for almost two years now, and it has been a tough, emotional, and sometimes lonely road. Nevertheless, my determination, passion for change, openness to new emotions, willingness to love again, and yearning to have a relationship with God has been my driving force.

I thank God daily that I'm not where I was, and I welcome wherever He takes me. My relationship with my parents is the best it has ever been, and I continue to make the effort right along with them for continuous growth and communication. It took a long time and a lot of effort to get to where we are now but, despite the road, I've been nothing but grateful for the journey. After our family forum and them speaking their peace, I left all the burden and pain of the past in that room that night. I refused to carry it anymore and I did not have to. I spoke my truth, they listened and apologized. They spoke their truth; I listened and accepted the apology. We vowed to move forward in a better and newfound way, prayed, and left it there. The relationship I have with my parents now is one that I used to dream of. I am blessed that I was able to acknowledge, release, and grow from all the past hurt and pain I endured and kept inside.

❤

Your condition determines your eligibility for your position! My previous condition was toxic and miserably broken. How on earth was I ever eligible for the position of being someone's wife? A successful, loving, submissive, caring, supportive, God-fearing wife? As a woman or man, your present condition will come out whether you want it to or not. On a team, personal conditions may be hard to figure out because play time is limited, and you have more than one person to sub in and out for the same position. Subsequently, with one-on-one activities, your qualifications/skills will appear within seconds of the first half, inning, or quarter. Make sure you're eligible before applying; trust me, it saves you and the other person in the long run!

I once heard a pastor say, "Remove the ripples before they become a flood; remove the hindrance that's stopping your flow; that lack of flow in your life may be a probable cause to issue a search warrant for your heart!" Allow me to cue the organist so I can shout right here! Search within yourself and question those highs and lows of life. What's stopping your flow? I am now on to a great flow of love, self-acceptance, and complete personal healing because I acted on removing the blockage.

I am currently dating, and I went into it open-minded. No lie, I had hesitations and was in my head a lot, but then I quickly reminded myself of what I wanted and where I didn't want to revert to. He's a great guy! I authentically love him and everything that makes him the unique being that he is! With God, a healed heart, and a healed mind, I am ready for my future!

Who knows, I may have 5 marriages before 40! And this one will LAST!

"The patterns in your life will determine the difference between the destruction of your life or the construction of it. It's up to you to choose" (Jakes Roberts, 2017).

# I CHOSE TO HEAL!

# ENCOURAGEMENT / AFFIRMATIONS

♡ Get what YOU need!
♡ Do what is best for YOU!
♡ Care less about what irrelevant people think!
♡ Lean on God!
♡ Get a journal!
♡ Express YOUrself!
♡ Be true to YOU!
♡ Be open to forgive!
♡ Be open to love!
♡ Choose YOU!
♡ Set standards!
♡ Set goals!
♡ Never settle!
♡ Trust God!
♡ Trust the process!
♡ Live intentionally!
♡ YOU are worth it!
♡ Celebrate YOU!
♡ Speak life!
♡ Love wins!
♡ YOU win some, YOU lose some!
♡ Your healing is exactly that, YOURS!
♡ Never feel ashamed about YOUR journey, we are all on one!

♥ No one is perfect but God, mistakes will happen!

♥ Don't stay down, get up!

♥ This is MY Exodus!

♥ Be grateful for the downfalls!

♥ God's will should be Your will!

♥ If HE allows it, embrace it with dignity and go forth!

♥ YOUR best is yet to come!

♥ Be encouraged!

♥ Hurt people, hurt people!

♥ Healing requires being uncomfortable, keep pushing!

♥ HEAL!!!

# ABOUT THE AUTHOR

Takenya Mims grew up in Memphis, TN and now resides in Houston, TX. She is a proud aunt of two nephews and is a godmother to four girls and three boys. Her favorite pastime is organizing, journaling, and watching the Golden Girls. She revels in being at home and relaxing at every free opportunity. Being a lover of water, she enjoys traveling to places with beaches and clean sand. She values her life's experiences and loves sharing her journey with others.

Made in the USA
Monee, IL
23 September 2020